KINGDOM TRAILBLAZERS

A Practical Guide For
Visionary Leadership

I.R. Womack

Copyright © 2022 I.R. Womack
Kingdom Trailblazers

Scriptures marked AMP are taken from the AMPLIFIED BIBLE (AMP): Scripture taken from the AMPLIFIED® BIBLE, Copyright © 1954, 1958, 1962, 1964, 1965, 1987 by the Lockman Foundation Used by Permission. (www.Lockman.org)

Scriptures marked NLT are taken from the HOLY BIBLE, NEW LIVING TRANSLATION (NLT): Scriptures taken from the HOLY BIBLE, NEW LIVING TRANSLATION, Copyright© 1996, 2004, 2007 by Tyndale House Foundation. Used by permission of Tyndale House Publishers, Inc., Carol Stream, Illinois 60188. All rights reserved. Used by permission.

Scriptures marked KJV are taken from the KING JAMES VERSION (KJV): KING JAMES VERSION, public domain.

Scriptures marked NIV are taken from the NEW INTERNATIONAL VERSION (NIV): Scripture taken from THE HOLY BIBLE, NEW INTERNATIONAL VERSION ®. Copyright© 1973, 1978, 1984, 2011 by Biblica, Inc.™. Used by permission of Zondervan

Scriptures marked NKJV are taken from the NEW KING JAMES VERSION (NKJV): Scripture taken from the NEW KING JAMES VERSION®. Copyright© 1982 by Thomas Nelson, Inc. Used by permission. All rights reserved.

"Scripture taken from *THE MESSAGE*. Copyright © 1993, 1994, 1995, 1996, 2000, 2001, 2002. Used by permission of NavPress Publishing Group."

"Scripture quotations taken from the (NASB®) New American Standard Bible®, Copyright © 1960, 1971, 1977, 1995, 2020 by The Lockman Foundation. Used by permission. All rights reserved. www.lockman.org"

Scripture quotations marked (PHPS) are taken from The New Testament in Modern English, copyright © 1958, 1959, 1960 J.B. Phillips and 1947, 1952, 1955, 1957 The Macmillian Company, New York. Used by permission. All rights reserved.

All rights reserved. No part of this book may be used or reproduced without written permission.

Alpha Book Publishing
info@alphabookpublishing.com

ISBN: 978-1-7372942-9-0

TABLE OF CONTENTS

Introduction 1

Chapter 1:   What is a Kingdom Trailblazer? 4

Chapter 2:   Anointed to Impact the Marketplace 30

Chapter 3:   Imagination: Can You See It? 46

Chapter 4:   Creativity 52

Chapter 5:   Trailblazing Faith 65

Chapter 6:   Risk Takers 73

Chapter 7:   Team-Building 81

Chapter 8:   Legacy: Laying the Foundation for Future
             Generations 89

Conclusion 95

References 103

OTHER BOOKS BY I.R. WOMACK

Fivefold Ministry Basic Training:

Understanding the distinct roles and functions of apostles, prophets, evangelists, pastors and teachers

Deliverance Ministry Basic Training:

Lear how to cast out demons & set the captives free

Prayers That Destroy Depression:

Prayers that break depression
and bring supernatural peace

Prayers That Ignite the Gifts of the Spirit:

Ignite and Increase Your Spiritual Gifts

SERVICES BY I.R. WOMACK
Alpha Book Publishing

Have an idea for a book?

Been working on a book but can't seem to get it done?

Have a finished manuscript and need help getting it published?

I'm here to help!

I Help Christian authors, speakers and business professionals write and publish their books in about 90 days to impact lives, grow their audiences and create new income streams.

At Alpha Book Publishing, we work with our writers every step of the way on their literary journey, helping to bring out the most from their work. From an idea and rough draft to editing and publication, Alpha Book Publishing helps our authors produce high-quality, thought-provoking and inspiring books.

Our services include ghostwriting, editing, proofreading, book cover design, marketing, branding, audience building and more! Because our primary focus is on Christian writers, we understand how to craft a polished and professional book that connects with their target audience and opens doors for new opportunities.

If you're ready to write and publish your book, I would love to help! Visit us today www.alphabookpublishing.com to review our packages and set up a free consultation.

INTRODUCTION

The Rise of the Kingdom Trailblazers

> *"Therefore go and make disciples of all nations, baptizing them in the name of the Father and of the Son and of the Holy Spirit, and teaching them to obey everything I have commanded you..."* (Matthew 28:19-20, NIV)

To fulfill the Great Commission in a fast-paced and ever-changing world, it is paramount that Believers are adaptable and innovative in their approach to engaging the world with the message of Christ and demonstrating the Kingdom in everyday situations. To meet the task at hand, the Lord is raising up Kingdom trailblazers and sending them to every sector and segment of society to do great exploits, create a Kingdom culture, and evangelize the world through their influence. These Kingdom trailblazers are an elite group of emissaries who are God's agents of change. Their mandate is to ensure that the Church remains on the cutting edge and continues to affect culture on the 7 mountains of societal influence: Education, Business, Family, Arts & Entertainment, Religion, Media, and Government.

The Purpose of this Book

The purpose of this book is to activate the trailblazing dimension in your life and provide a blueprint for you to launch and strategically impact your sphere of influence. It's designed to help you tap into your God-given abilities and align them with your purpose so that you can make a unique and significant contribution in your field for the glory of God.

It is my hope that by reading this book, you will be empowered and equipped to be a more effective Kingdom ambassador who helps bring the Church back to cultural relevance. You will learn Kingdom principles to help you become a creative force for change and advancement with your skills, gifts, and talents. Your Kingdom vision and perspective will be enhanced, allowing you to think more strategically about how you can make a difference in your field while fulfilling your unique role in the body of Christ.

Those who have lost momentum in their lives, businesses, or ministries will be reignited and propelled forward to fulfill their vision and destiny with fresh insights and a newfound vigor. You'll be challenged and inspired to step out of your comfort zone to achieve new levels of success and prosperity. You'll be equipped to be a major force for the Kingdom by blending godly leadership and Kingdom lifestyle principles with effective Kingdom strategies.

We will begin with a comprehensive look into the Kingdom trailblazer's DNA profile. We will then highlight and expound on key attributes that are indispensable for the success of a Kingdom trailblazer's mission. Finally, we'll conclude with powerful affirmations to help stir up and activate the trailblazing dimension in your life.

To get the most out of this book, you should not only read it to gain head knowledge. Instead, take the presented concepts and develop a purposeful plan of implementation. Doing so will enable you to prove to be a trailblazer second to none in your respective field and will help you fulfill your Kingdom mission with high honors.

It is my honor and privilege to walk this journey with you as we discover and unleash the power of your God-given potential. You're on track to make a significant contribution in the world that will be felt for generations to come.

Let the journey begin.

Chapter 1

WHAT IS A KINGDOM TRAILBLAZER?

Kingdom trailblazers are innovators, visionaries, and influencers who lead the way forward in their fields, operating by Kingdom principles and values. Simultaneously, they leave a lasting impression on the seven mountains of societal influence while bringing glory to Christ as His noble ambassadors (if you'd like a comprehensive study of the seven mountains and how the Church is called to impact them, I suggest you read another book I've published, "SPEAK TO THE MOUNTAINS — Prayers & Prophetic Decrees for the 7 Mountains of Cultural Influence").

As revolutionary change agents, they dare to dream and push boundaries. They've been tested, purified by the Refiner's fire, and empowered by God to lead the Kingdom charge, resulting in significant advancements, innovations, breakthroughs and paradigm shifts.

Daniel was a man who did everything with a spirit of excellence. He was noted as one who had insight, intelligence and wisdom (see Daniel 5:11). He could interpret dreams and solve difficult problems (see Daniel 5:12). Daniel's outstanding resume opened the door for him to become one of the highest ranking officials in Babylon and transform the religious landscape:

One day, Kingdom Belshazzar gave one thousand of his nobles a great banquet and drank wine with them. He then gave orders to bring in the gold and silver goblets that his father Nebuchadnezzar had taken from the temple in Jerusalem so that he and his nobles, wives and concubines might drink from them.

So, they brought in the gold goblets that had been taken from the temple of God in Jerusalem, and they all drank from them. As they drank their wine, they praised their idols. Suddenly, the fingers of a human hand appeared and wrote on the plaster of the wall, near the lampstand in the royal palace. The king watched as the hand wrote. He became so frightened that his face became pale. His knees knocked together, and his legs became weak.

The king then summoned the enchanters, astrologers and diviners to explain the meaning of the writing on the wall. None of the other wise men in the kingdom could interpret this dream—but Daniel could. So, the king richly rewarded Daniel and favored him above all the other princes and royal officials. He was promoted to the third highest ruler in the kingdom and greatly prospered.

If you look closely at Daniel's life, you'll see that he was a trailblazer second to none. He had the ability to see beneath the surface of matters and fathom what others could not grasp. He was a visionary leader who influenced others with his ideas, insights, and uncompromising faith (see Daniel 1:3-16, 2:1-49, 3:19-34). As a result, he was able to create a religious and cultural shift in the kingdom and bring about lasting change:

> *Then King Darius wrote to all the nations and peoples of every language in all the earth:*
>
> *"May you prosper greatly!*
>
> *"I issue a decree that in every part of my kingdom people must fear and reverence the God of Daniel.*
>
> *"For he is the living God and he endures forever; his kingdom will not be destroyed, his dominion will never end. He rescues and he saves; he performs signs and wonders in the heavens and*

on the earth. He has rescued Daniel from the power of the lions" (Daniel 6: 25-27 NIV).

Like Daniel, Kingdom trailblazers today carry out their purposes and missions with a spirit of excellence — at the highest level of integrity and commitment. They set themselves apart through their work ethic, creative ideas, insight, foresight, and faith. As a result, they win the respect of their colleagues, superiors, and those whom they influence, as the Kingdom advances.

Vessels of Honor

"But in a great house there are not only vessels of gold and silver, but also of wood and clay, some for honor and some for dishonor. Therefore if anyone cleanses himself from the latter, he will be a vessel for honor, sanctified and useful for the Master, prepared for every good work" (2 Timothy 2:20-21, NKJV).

Many Christians today make it their business to go unnoticed. They are content to play it safe and not ruffle any feathers. Rarely do they take a stand for what they believe, challenge the status quo, or try to relate to people in the world in order to reach them for Christ.

They are generally satisfied with living out their lives in the shadows, embracing mediocrity and declining opportunities for greatness. They find it much easier to stay in their own bubbles than to reach out into the world and make a difference for the glory of God.

Kingdom trailblazers are a different breed. As vessels of honor, they willingly embark upon special missions for King Jesus to accomplish His will and gain glory for Him. They seize the initiative with a sense of urgency about their mission and a passion for leaving the world better than they found it. They exhibit a strong commitment to the Great Commission as they demonstrate the character and power of God in everyday situations.

Let it Flow

> *"He that believeth on me, as the scripture hath said, out of his belly shall flow rivers of living water"* (John 7:38, KJV).

Kingdom trailblazers are conduits for the Spirit of God to manifest. They know how to flow with the Holy Spirit and release His creativity, wisdom, and power to bring new life and abundant blessings to the people and places where they serve. They are bridge-builders who understand how to love people, relate to them, and connect them with Christ.

Kingdom trailblazers are passionate about operating in the gifts of the Spirit. They understand that when they move in these spiritual gifts, problems are solved, objectives are achieved, and the Holy Spirit touches and transforms lives.

Here are descriptions for the nine gifts of the Spirit from my booklet, *Prayers That Ignite the Gifts of the Spirit*:

The Word of Wisdom—a supernatural provision of divine counsel or right application of knowledge. There are numerous examples of the word of wisdom in the Scriptures. Whenever you see an instruction given before a supernatural event takes place, this is the word of wisdom in operation. This gift is not to be confused with general wisdom that can be attained by education or experience; rather, it's a supernatural impartation that comes directly from the Holy Spirit. The word of wisdom speaks to a specific problem, situation or circumstance and provides the solution. It's the revealed will of God, not just another suggestion. The trailblazer who operates in the gift of wisdom will not have to guess, speculate, or struggle to determine the next right move. The Holy Spirit will give him very specific direction and instruction—even if it defies logic. The gift of wisdom is not given to produce a person who has all the answers, but rather one who knows how to receive and act upon the instructions provided by God.

The Word of Knowledge—a divine revelation of facts, past or present, which were not learned through the efforts of the natural mind. It is the supernatural revelation of details, facts, and information about people, circumstances, or events, unknowable except through Divine communication to the human spirit. This gift is a powerful tool for the trailblazer because the Holy Spirit reveals the right information at the right time to overcome obstacles or difficulties, or to confirm to others that God is operating in the situation. Kingdom trailblazers don't have to figure everything out for themselves; by the word of knowledge, they can receive accurate and detailed information from the Holy Spirit to assist them in their personal pursuits or ministry to others.

The Discerning of Spirits—the supernatural ability to recognize the identity, personality, or state of the spirit behind various manifestations. It also involves the ability to detect the source of human thought or motivation by discerning the spiritual source behind the idea or reason for doing something. This supernatural recognition can come by means of inner perception or by seeing into the spirit realm. This spiritual gift enables you to distinguish the presence and activity of the Holy Spirit, angels, human spirits—even evil spirits. This supernatural discernment is invaluable for the Kingdom trailblazer as it enables you to perceive when something is or isn't of God. It also enables you to see through deception and uncover spirits that oppress, dominate, or control people and places.

The Gifts of Healing—the supernatural ability to impart healing to the physical body, mind, and emotions. This is important to the Kingdom trailblazer because it enables you to bring wholeness and freedom from destructive patterns, generational curses, various infirmities, and other types of demonic interferences in people's lives. Some of your greatest supporters and most faithful team members will be people who have been healed in some way by the power of God through your ministry.

The Working of Miracles—a spiritual gift that enables an individual to work with God outside the laws of nature. It's the supernatural ability to bring needed solutions into existence when no natural explanation exists and no natural solution is available. In order to break through tough and seemingly unbreakable ground, this supernatural miracle-working ability is invaluable. Heavenly assistance will be granted to the Kingdom trailblazer to operate outside the laws of nature to bring solutions, breakthroughs, and turnarounds that ordinarily would be impossible.

The Gift of Faith — the supernatural ability to believe for the impossible in a given situation. The gift of faith is not to be confused with general faith; it's the very faith of God. God's faith will always produce supernatural results. As a pioneer, you may encounter situations that don't make sense to you, or which the natural mind can't understand. You may also find yourself in situations where the odds are stacked against you, and you can't see a way forward. The gift of faith will enable you to believe for the impossible to take place — and it will!

The Gift of Prophecy — the supernatural ability to know and speak the mind and counsel of God. It can involve forth-telling a divinely inspired message or giving an inspired message pertaining to a future event. The purpose of this gift is to edify, exhort, and comfort God's people. This gift has extreme value to the Kingdom trailblazer. Like Nehemiah, who raised a team to help rebuild the walls of Jerusalem, you'll need to assemble and equip teams to accomplish most Kingdom initiatives. This gift will help you to motivate, inspire, and point the way forward with a divinely inspired word.

Tongues and Interpretation of Tongues — the divine enablement to speak a language that the speaker does not know in order to minister to an individual or group of people who understand the language being spoken. It also enables the orator to speak in an unknown or heavenly language that requires the gift of the interpretation of tongues to reveal the meaning of the message. Although perhaps not as commonplace as the other gifts of the Spirit, the Kingdom trailblazer can benefit immensely by having the ability to speak in tongues and interpret them. This gift will help you explode into new realms of Kingdom authority that you've never experienced before. It can also release revelation from God that is needed to produce cutting-edge technologies, systems, and strategies that advance the Kingdom in the various sectors of society.

Kingdom Strategists

"Good planning and hard work lead to prosperity..."
(Proverbs 21:5 NLT).

Strategic planning is the process by which an individual determines their goals, then generates and evaluates options to reach those goals. Kingdom trailblazers are master strategists who know how to devise plans that will yield the greatest results. Creating and implementing a strategic plan is an invaluable skill for Kingdom trailblazers. They must be focused and purposeful but flexible in their approach to issues that arise along the way. Their plans will lead to success, financial increase, and monumental breakthroughs. Strategic planning in Kingdom service should include the following components:

1. A clearly-defined vision: If you don't know where you're going, any path will take you there. Kingdom strategists see their destination from afar and chart a course to get there efficiently.

"Where there is no vision [no revelation of God and His word], the people are unrestrained..." (Proverbs 29:18, AMP).

2. A comprehensive plan of action: A written plan that includes specific goals, timetables for achieving them, evaluation processes, steps to monitor progress, contact lists, and material needs. The plan should also have a provision for a realistic budget, including funding sources if needed. Finally, this plan must also include contingencies for obstacles that are likely to arise along the way.

> *"Write the vision; make it plain..."* (Habakkuk 2:2 ESV); *"Is there anyone here who, planning to build a new house, doesn't first sit down and figure the cost so you'll know if you can complete it? If you only get the foundation laid and then run out of money, you're going to look pretty foolish. Everyone passing by will poke fun at you..."* (Luke 14:28, MSG).

3. Team check-ins: It's important to gather the team members regularly to monitor progress, assess the current status of tasks, share insights, and refine the plan as needed. During these meetings, you should look for what's working as well as what's not working, and determine what needs to be modified. You should also look for ideas on how the plan might be more effectively executed.

> *"Where there is no counsel, the people fall; But in the multitude of counselors there is safety"* (Proverbs 11:14, NKJV).

4. Prayer and reflection: Kingdom strategists are deep thinkers who make calculated moves. They prayerfully seek

God's wisdom, understanding and insight into how to proceed. They seek God's will for their lives and His Kingdom work, then receive revelation knowledge that they can apply to the plan.

> *"Trust in and rely confidently on the Lord with all your heart And do not rely on your own insight or understanding. In all your ways know and acknowledge and recognize Him, And He will make your paths straight and smooth [removing obstacles that block your way]"* (Proverbs 3: 5-6, AMP).

5. Perseverance: A plan is of little benefit if it's not carried out to completion. Kingdom strategists have an unwavering determination to fulfill their commissions from God regardless of the adverse circumstances that may arise.

> *"Therefore, my beloved brothers and sisters, be steadfast, immovable, always excelling in the work of the Lord [always doing your best and doing more than is needed], being continually aware that your labor [even to the point of exhaustion] in the Lord is not futile nor wasted [it is never without purpose]"* (1 Corinthians 15:58, AMP).

As the plans of Kingdom strategists are executed, the body of Christ is being equipped to take the lead in establishing systems and structures that will sustain the Church, advance

Kingdom values and principles, and usher in a new move of God.

Power to Bring Change

> *"Let your light so shine before men, that they may see your good works, and glorify your Father which is in heaven"* (Matthew 5:16, KJV).

Kingdom trailblazers are change agents who shift the climate of the environment around them to bring about revival and reform. They challenge cultural norms, overcome opposition, and persist in their efforts to bring about godly change. They are catalysts for transformation, reaching into the hearts of people and systems to tear down strongholds and change lives. Those who witness Kingdom trailblazers in action are often inspired to improve their own lives. They want what Kingdom trailblazers have!

Martin Luther was one of the most well-known reformers in Church history who dared to challenge the status quo and strove to bring reform to the Church in the 16th century. Luther's main concern was the Catholic doctrine's focus on indulgences (paying money so your soul could be saved). He contended that people should receive forgiveness for their sins through faith alone, not by paying money or doing penance as if they deserved it based on how many good deeds they had done.

On October 31, 1517, Luther posted his 95 Theses challenging the Church on the door of the Castle Church in Wittenberg, Germany. Rather than remaining quiet and avoiding conflict, he challenged his peers and their teachings, which caused many to stand tall for truth and reform.

The 95 Theses spread throughout Europe and eventually led to the reform within the Catholic Church. In addition, Luther's efforts helped lead to what is today known as Protestantism, which includes some of the major denominations such as the Lutheran, Baptist, Methodist, and Presbyterian Churches.

However, Luther's efforts did not come without severe opposition and persecution. He was excommunicated from the Roman Catholic Church in 1521 by Pope Leo X. When he refused to recant his writings at the Diet of Worms, he was declared an outlaw and a heretic by Roman Emperor Charles V. Luther was forced into hiding at Wartburg Castle to escape assassination. Yet, he persevered in the face of persecution and continued to call others into action for reform until his death on February 18, 1546.

Martin Luther was a forward thinker who made other notable culture-shifting changes in his lifetime:

Music—Luther used the emotionally captivating power of music to reach people from every social class and background for Christ. A singer, songwriter, and musician in his own right, he wrote a myriad of hymns and instituted congregational singing in the Church.

Women's Empowerment—women were not well respected in the pre-Reformation Church and were seen as inferior to men. This began to shift gradually after celibacy laws lifted and clergy could now marry. The wives of these men began to share in their husbands' pastoral duties and participated in religious activities such as prayer sessions and Bible study groups. Many helped take care of parishioners who needed guidance and distributed food during times when it was scarce. With time, women were able to become ordained ministers of the Gospel.

The Luther Bible—Luther wanted to make sure every German-speaking person could read the Bible for themselves, so he translated it into their language. By 1534, with the assistance of others, Luther had succeeded in translating both the Old and New Testaments from Hebrew and Greek versions of the text, which were intended for scholars only.

Like Martin Luther, many Kingdom trailblazers will have a burning passion for reform and will endure severe hardships to see positive change come about as the Kingdom of God is advanced.

Will you be one of these reformers?

Will you be a Kingdom trailblazer?

Exploring New Frontiers

> *"It is the glory of God to conceal a matter; to search out a matter is the glory of kings"* (Proverbs 25:3, NIV).

Kingdom Trailblazers are intrepid explorers and discoverers. With a pioneering spirit, they seek to expand the boundaries of knowledge or achievement for the advancement of the Kingdom. They employ their focused vision to accomplish an ambitious goal for Kingdom impact; they go beyond conventional thinking or traditional ways to shake things up and affect their environment in new ways. Kingdom trailblazers have an appetite for new, bold, and innovative thinking that moves culture forward while advancing the cause of Christ.

Kingdom trailblazers are revolutionary leaders who stir up the settled, complacent, and stagnant. They are catalysts of change who seek to upset the status quo in order to reconstruct it into a better way that glorifies God and meets the needs of people. They have a vision for better ways to do things and they take massive action to bring about said vision.

They believe that every challenge is an opportunity. They use their bold, imaginative, and creative approach to solve problems. Courageously, they take steps to break with old, ineffective models, forging a daring new future. They lead with passion and conviction, always taking God's heart and His priorities into consideration in their decision-making.

Everything for the Glory of God

> *"So whether you eat or drink or whatever you do, do it all for the glory of God"* (1 Corinthians 10:31, NIV).

There's a wide chasm separating the sacred and the secular in modern times. This is a construct of man. In Biblical times things were not this way. God desired every aspect of life to be infused with His presence and glory. Kingdom Trailblazers seek to break down those cultural and societal constructs that separate the sacred from the secular. This is why the 7 Mountain Mandate resonates so deeply with them; it focuses on making a Kingdom impact in every area of life. Therefore, Kingdom trailblazers do not compartmentalize their faith. Instead, they express their faith in every situation so that God's glory can manifest in all they do.

Breaking New Ground

A term closely associated with a trailblazer is "pioneer." Throughout this book, we will be using the words trailblazer and pioneer interchangeably. According to the Miriam Webster dictionary, a pioneer is a person or group that originates or helps open up a new line of thought or activity or a new method or technical development. It is also defined as one of the first to settle in a territory. An individual with a pioneering spirit is not content with the status quo and embarks on a mission to do something new or different.

Pioneers go before others as forerunners to lay down new paths. They clear away obstacles and build bridges for others to follow in their footsteps. They are not afraid of being the first ones into uncharted territory, and they have an uncanny ability to see what needs to be done before anyone else does.

Pioneers also break new ground by opening up a line of thought or activity that is innovative and brings fresh air into an industry or area of society that is stagnant and in need of a new perspective.

Jesus the *Archegos*

"You killed the author of life, but God raised him from the dead. We are witnesses of this" (Acts 3:15, NIV).

The first and foremost Biblical example of a pioneer is none other than the Living Word Himself—Jesus Christ. John W. Rittenbaugh eloquently states:

"In the scripture referenced above, Jesus is called the author of life. The word author is translated from the Greek word "archegos" and has the sense of being "originator," someone who starts or begins something. An archegos is one who leads the way so that others may follow. It can also be translated "trailblazer," "scout," or "pioneer," and so it indicates one who leads into battle, blazes a trail, sets a pattern, one who initiates and guides."

"An archegos can found a school that others may follow him into learning. An archegos can found a city that others may dwell in. An archegos can blaze a trail that others may follow. An archegos can begin a family that others may be born into it.

In Hebrews 2:10, Jesus is called the archegos of our salvation. He blazed the trail! He set the pattern! He entered into God's Family that others may follow! And in blazing the trail, setting the pattern, entering God's Kingdom – He too was perfect!" (John W. Ritenbaugh)

Blazing New Trails

With a pioneering spirit, a trailblazer carries out a Kingdom mandate in whatever field or industry they've been sent. They blaze new trails for God's Kingdom on earth to advance its interests in every area of society. Kingdom pioneers are highly inventive, producing groundbreaking methodologies, inventions, products, concepts, systems, and designs that push Kingdom culture forward while solving complex problems and bringing practical solutions to society. They are not just church leaders. They can be inventors, founders, builders, CEOs, teachers or thought leaders, even parents, etc. Their efforts help shape our spiritual, social, cultural, and economic landscape. They are innovative and bold in their approach to their life's work. They break new ground — often in the midst of opposition, persecution, ridicule, or disbelief.

Johannes Gutenberg was a German blacksmith who revolutionized the printing press in the mid 15th century. Although China had developed a version of a printing press centuries earlier, Gutenberg's model was the first that could mass-produce books inexpensively. This accelerated the spread of knowledge and even helped kick the Renaissance period into high gear, as classic texts could now be republished in record time at a much lower cost. The printing press also enabled the message of Christ to explode all over the world, expanding Biblical knowledge for everyone who wanted it—without having to rely solely on the interpretations or opinions of clerical leaders.

Gutenberg's contribution to society is felt to this very day, as his invention enabled people throughout history to encounter spiritual concepts they may have never encountered otherwise. He's a notable pioneer because of how he spearheaded a new system that has been influential to generations for the expansion of God's Kingdom. He was not limited by tradition or what was done before him. He did not allow himself to be contained within anyone's defined limits. He had the grace and creativity, drive, and determination that enabled him to spark a technological revolution that would change the world.

The Protestant Reformation owes much to Gutenberg's invention. This cutting-edge technology allowed Martin Luther's 95 Theses to go viral! Without the mass production and distribution of Luther's message, it's possible that his movement would have failed to gain the momentum needed to influence the masses and spark the events that propelled the Protestant Reformation.

There is no doubt that Gutenberg's role was key in spreading God's Word to the masses and sparking major advancements and reform—and so it is with Kingdom pioneers today! They are those who think outside of the box, finding ways to spread or exemplify God's Word to a larger audience using new technologies, tools, or methods.

The internet, social media, podcasts, media outlets, and video sharing sites like YouTube are just a few of the new "printing presses" that God is using to get His Word out to an ever-expanding audience. Kingdom pioneers blaze trails in these and other avenues of culture every day!

Revelation Knowledge

Kingdom pioneers are revolutionary in their way of thinking to bring new ideas and change into a situation. They've been given revelation knowledge from God, which gives them a profound understanding of their mission and purpose, serving as a spiritual compass to ensure they remain aligned with their destinies.

Kingdom pioneers are constantly moving forward into new territories to further the cause of Christ. In a continually changing and adapting world, Kingdom pioneers depend on divine insight and foresight to remain on the cutting edge and to lead the path forward.

The apostle Paul is another great example of a Kingdom pioneer. He was educated in the law and customs of Israel by Gamaliel, one of the leading rabbis of the first century. He became a Pharisee of the highest order and far surpassed his peers in his meticulous observance of the law (see Galatians 1:14). He was very zealous for the Jewish faith, to the point of persecuting Christians with a vengeance. But after encountering the risen Jesus on the road to Damascus, he had a radical change of heart and mind. He began preaching that Jesus was the Messiah and Savior of all—Gentiles included.

While his Jewish counterparts were requiring Gentiles to become Jewish in order to be saved, Paul received the revelation that Christ's death and resurrection made salvation available to everyone without having to convert to Judaism. Circumcision, dietary restrictions, and the whole "works-based salvation" system of religion practiced by many Jews at the time were no longer necessary for salvation. This was a very radical message and caused a stir among many who felt that Paul's message was heresy.

The mission Paul was given was undoubtedly difficult. Still, he persevered and took bold steps in obedience to the revelation he received from the Lord, eventually leading to an unprecedented Gospel explosion that penetrated the very heart of the Roman Empire. Despite the great danger, threats against his life, and opposition from his own people, he continued to traverse the ancient world, preaching the Gospel, planting churches, raising leaders, and breaking down traditional religious systems.

Breaking Out of the Box of Traditionalism

In Romans 12:2 JBP, Paul the apostle admonishes us not to let the world squeeze us into its mold. This scripture resonates deeply within the spirit of Kingdom pioneers; they refuse to allow the box of traditionalism or social norms to dictate their way of thinking or mode of operation. Instead, they are visionary trendsetters who know that living out a radical faith in unconventional ways is what God had in mind for them and those they lead.

Henry Ford once said, *"If I had asked my customers what they wanted they would have said a faster horse."* This is exactly why a Kingdom pioneer thinks out of the box — to make sizable strides forward, they must be able to see what others do not and bring it into existence.

NOTES

Chapter 2

ANOINTED TO IMPACT THE MARKETPLACE

"But remember the Lord your God, for it is he who gives you the ability to produce wealth..."
Deuteronomy 8:18, NIV

Kingdom trailblazers are innovative thinkers who take thoughts, ideas, and concepts and create something tangible that is not only profitable, but also serves a greater purpose. They aren't afraid to bring new methods or systems that are unconventional to the marketplace. They blaze trails for Kingdom expansion by inventing new platforms and technologies that broaden the horizon of Kingdom impact and influence.

The Knights Templar: Economic Trailblazers

The Knights Templar was a monastic order of Christian warriors who changed the landscape of the European economy and society during the 12th and 13th centuries. The order was formed in 1119 and grew rapidly in membership, power, and wealth.

After Christian military fighters seized control of Jerusalem from Muslim forces in 1099, Christians from all over Western Europe would travel to the Holy Land to visit various sacred sites. This was a treacherous pilgrimage as they had to pass through Muslim-controlled territories. Many people were robbed and killed on this journey.

In response, the Knights Templar was formed under the leadership of Hugh de Payens, vowing to protect and defend pilgrims making the migration to the Holy Land. With King Baldwin II's blessing, they set up headquarters in a section of the royal palace on the Temple Mount. The Knights Templar progressively expanded its duties from protecting pilgrims to defending Crusader states against Islamic armies. They became known for being brave and highly skilled warriors who would not retreat unless significantly outnumbered.

Although they are best known for their military prowess, only about ten percent of the Knights Templar actually engaged in warfare. Instead, as astute businessmen, most of their work focused on economic impact—they were bankers, financiers, and traders. In this capacity, along with large donations of land and money, they became one of the wealthiest groups in Europe. They amassed what would be equivalent to several billion dollars today. This money was then used to finance various endeavors, including military campaigns in the Holy Land, building castles, cathedrals, and monasteries, and constructing roads.

The Knights Templar is also credited as the first organization to establish an international banking system. Since the Christians making their pilgrimage to the Holy Land often carried large sums of money, the Knights Templar developed a financial system where the pilgrims could deposit funds in their home countries and receive a letter of credit. When they arrived in the Holy Land, they could then withdraw funds from a Templar preceptory (a type of early bank), reducing the risk of being robbed. On a grander scale, the Knights Templar controlled such vast amounts of wealth that they began issuing loans to kings and nobles of Europe, which further increased their wealth and political influence.

Like the Knights Templar, many Kingdom trailblazers today are called to innovate and excel in the area of business and finance. They are developing new platforms and technologies that expand the horizon of Kingdom impact and influence in the world. As they utilize their unique skills and resources to impact their society, they're changing the course of history.

The Entrepreneurial Spirit

Living radically for Christ doesn't just occur in our religious gatherings or service-oriented ministries. It is also demonstrated in our marketplace engagements as we work hard and blaze trails with excellence, using our God-given gifts and abilities in service to humanity.

Many trailblazers have an entrepreneurial spirit, which leads them to create businesses, products, and services that fulfill a need in the marketplace. They are passionate about their work and contribute to society by establishing Kingdom-centered initiatives and enterprises. They are willing to take a stand that may cost them money and even their reputations, but they do so because of their commitment to the Kingdom of God. Kingdom trailblazers live in the world but not by it; they are brilliant individuals capable of achieving great success. They are leaders who know how to attract others who want to follow them on a common mission.

To Kingdom trailblazers, there is no need for a "Plan B." They believe God has called them to create something new and innovative—a blueprint that will change how things are done, impacting their community, nation, and world. Kingdom trailblazers work hard to get results; they leave nothing on the field and finish what they start. Their spiritual integrity produces hard work and honest business dealings; they are transparent in their relationships, being true to themselves and others.

A notable Kingdom entrepreneur who blazed new trails was John D. Rockefeller Sr. He founded Standard Oil in 1870, which was once the largest oil refinery in the world, controlling over 90% of the American petroleum industry. He made his fortune by developing innovative methods to produce kerosene and fuel oil while implementing cost-cutting measures that made his company even more profitable. Rockefeller's relentless pursuit of efficiency and innovation led to new methods of utilizing discarded oil byproducts to create useful items such as lubricants, paints, and other products.

He ferociously and successfully competed against his rivals (some say to a fault), bringing about changes to the industry by pioneering what we know today as vertical integration. His philosophy in business was to seek out and win new customers, even if it meant temporarily losing money on each sale. He spent a lot of time and energy building and maintaining relationships with business partners, suppliers, and competitors. His goal was to build a profitable enterprise that would last for decades—and he did.

He believed his ability to produce wealth came from God, as he is quoted as saying, "I believe the power to make money is a gift from God..." To put his wealth in perspective, as of the date of this writing, the wealthiest person in the world is Elon Musk, with a net worth of about $286 billion. Adjusted for inflation, the highest estimates state that John D. Rockefeller's net worth would be approximately $400 billion, making him the wealthiest person in all of human history!

Kingdom Philanthropy

While Rockefeller is more known for his wealth and accomplishments in the business world, he was also a devout Baptist and churchman. Rockefeller read the Bible daily and led a Bible study group with his wife.

He believed in the importance of giving back and making a difference in society. Rockefeller lived by the creed that it was a moral obligation to share his wealth with others. He was a Kingdom philanthropist who used his business acumen and fortune to advance the cause of Christ, helping individuals in need as well as spearheading and supporting various Church-based initiatives and institutions.

At a time when discrimination and segregation were commonplace, Rockefeller's philanthropic donations and support helped improve the quality of education for African Americans and other minorities. Rockefeller believed in racial equality and donated millions of dollars to HBCUs (Historically Black Colleges and Universities) such as the Fisk University and Spelman College, which was named after his wife, Laura Spelman.

He held close to a Biblical principle found in Proverbs 11:4, which states, "*Riches do not profit in the day of wrath...*" Rockefeller believed that the more money one had, the greater responsibility one also obtained. In a noble effort to combat disease, John founded the Rockefeller Institute for Medical Research, which aimed to study and find cures for many ailments such as diabetes, syphilis, yellow fever, and heart disease. This was the first biomedical research center in the United States. From there, the institute expanded to become the Rockefeller University, located in New York City, and in 1959 they awarded its first doctoral degrees.

Like Rockefeller, I believe that God is raising many more Kingdom entrepreneurs that will have tremendous economic success. They will become Kingdom philanthropists and financiers who will use their business acumen, influence, and wealth on a massive scale to help the poor, advance the Kingdom of God, and change society for the better.

1 Timothy 6:17-19 gives us insight on how to steward our wealth and use it used for the glory of God:

> *"Command those who are rich in this present world not to be arrogant nor to put their hope in wealth, which is so uncertain, but to put their hope in God, who richly provides us with everything for our enjoyment. Command them to do good, to be rich in good deeds, and to be generous and willing to share. In this way, they will lay up treasure for themselves as a firm foundation for the coming age, so that they may take hold of the life that is truly life"* (1 Timothy 6:17-19, NIV).

Economic Justice

> *Thus says the Lord, "Do justice and righteousness, and deliver the one who has been robbed from the power of his oppressor...* (Jeremiah 22:3 NASB).

Economic justice is a necessary component of Kingdom Living. It's an ethical framework for building our economy, where the goal is to create a system that benefits every individual, including those who are marginalized, impoverished and discriminated against. Economic justice aims to redress issues such as:

- Unequal distribution of power and wealth within society, which leads to the concentration of wealth in the hands of a few.
- Unequal access to resources like capital and land, which contributes to poverty, hunger and homelessness.
- Inequitable distribution of labor in society, which leads to unemployment, low wages and slave labor.
- Inability to participate in the economy, which excludes certain groups from wealth creation and perpetuates poverty.
- Unequal access to education and professional training, which leads to low earning power and a lack of employment opportunities.
- Unequal access to health care, which increases vulnerability to illness and poverty.
- Political power that is not accountable to the community it represents, which leads to corruption and poor socioeconomic policies.

This list is not exhaustive, but it does give us a general idea of what economic justice seeks to accomplish. Kingdom trailblazers who understand what it means to execute economic justice will be at the forefront of helping to dismantle economic injustice in all forms. They will lead the charge that causes society's systems and structures to operate in a manner that benefits all, creating opportunities for everyone to thrive and prosper.

Madam C.J. Walker was a notable Kingdom entrepreneur who was a strong advocate for economic justice. She used her wealth and influence to empower people in need and establish systems that changed the lives of many. Born Sarah Breedlove on a cotton plantation to formerly enslaved parents, Walker overcame extreme adversity to become America's first self-made female millionaire. Through her business acuity and entrepreneurial spirit, she pioneered a hair care line for women of color which became immensely popular and profitable in the early 20th century.

In 1908, Madam CJ Walker founded the Lelia College of Beauty Culture to empower black women through economic development. Through this college, she created employment opportunities for thousands of women and provided them with professional training, enabling them to become entrepreneurs themselves. One of her brochures targeting ambitious black women stated, "Open your own shop; secure prosperity and freedom."

Because of state-sponsored discrimination, black women were relegated to menial, low-paying jobs. Walker was determined to change this and paid her employees more than 10X what they would otherwise have earned as domestic workers. This radically transformed the financial status and quality of life for thousands of black families all across the country.

Homeownership is one of the most important aspects of building wealth. During the Jim Crow era, discriminatory legislation and economic practices prevented black families from accessing bank loans to finance their homes. In response, Madam Walker used her wealth to personally provide financing for many black families allowing them to pay her back "when and what they could."

Madam CJ Walker's marketplace ministry, philanthropy and fight for justice and equality was an expression of her deeply rooted Christian faith. She was a member of the AME church that helped shape her worldview, impacting the way she conducted business and worked on the behalf of others. Her life was a living example of Jeremiah 22:3 as she delivered those who've been robbed from the power of their oppressors.

Like Madam CJ Walker, God is raising up many more Kingdom entrepreneurs to blaze trails in various sectors.

These individuals will use their vast resources and influence to help the poor and vulnerable, sow into individuals for personal development, establish innovative businesses and influence society with a practical demonstration of the Gospel.

12 Characteristics of Kingdom Entrepreneurs

What does it take to be a successful Kingdom entrepreneur? What personality traits should they have? Here is a shortlist of common characteristics that distinguish successful Kingdom entrepreneurs from dreamers:

1. **Purpose-driven:** Kingdom entrepreneurs serve a purpose bigger than themselves. They don't just want to make money; they want to impact other people's lives and help them enjoy a better quality of life. They are driven to fulfill a mission that has been given to them by God.
2. **Zeal:** Kingdom entrepreneurs are energetic and ambitious. They love what they do and do it with passion. They have an enthusiasm for their mission that is contagious and inspires others.
3. **Inventiveness:** The ability to discover new ways to solve existing problems is a critical skill that all

successful Kingdom entrepreneurs must possess. They must have a problem-solving mindset that employs creative thinking to develop innovative ideas and solutions.

4. **All-in attitude:** Kingdom entrepreneurs don't just dabble—they're all-in. They invest their time, energy, money, and resources into their mission. They refuse to give up when the going gets tough and resolve to persevere until they accomplish their objectives.

5. **Leadership:** In today's fast-paced global economy, entrepreneurial leadership has become an essential ingredient of success. Successful leaders must lead in many ways, including networking and developing strategic partnerships, recruiting talented team members, developing emerging leaders, implementing innovative growth strategies, communicating effectively across multiple channels, and managing change. It is essential for leaders to know what they are good at and leverage their strengths.

6. **Adaptability:** Some organizations have become so entrenched in their business models and ways of doing things that they cannot adapt quickly to the unpredictable dynamics of their industry. A great leader will create an environment where creativity,

innovation, and new ideas are embraced, so the organization can better adapt to a rapidly shifting business landscape while staying true to its vision, values, and strategic plan.

7. **Harness Technology:** Entrepreneurs who embrace technology and incorporate it into their business model find ways to expand capabilities, reduce costs, streamline the work process, better engage and serve their target audience, and increase profits. Technology is no longer an option: it is the superior way to reach people, get them involved, and build influence.

8. **Life-long Learners:** Entrepreneurs are always learning new things and surrounding themselves with those who challenge them and expand their thinking. It is a natural state of being for them. They are eager to learn new skills so they can be better leaders and contribute more to their ministries, companies, teams, customers, and communities.

9. **Resilience:** Business is risky. Most new businesses fail within the first five years, and it takes tenacity, resilience, and passion to keep going when things are not doing well. While it is good to know when you are in over your head and need to bring in reinforcements, the person with an entrepreneurial spirit maintains a

vision and keeps moving forward towards that vision. They learn from what doesn't work and persevere with a goal-oriented mindset while making adjustments in the right direction.

10. **Service-Driven:** Entrepreneurs are service-driven. This is an area where Christians should thrive, as we should be well acquainted with the concept of serving other people. Service-driven entrepreneurs ask, "What can I do to help or solve a problem?" They give of themselves sacrificially and focus on adding value to others.

11. **A Strong Work Ethic:** Entrepreneurs are highly motivated and have a strong work ethic. They maintain a sense of urgency for getting things done. They are achievement-oriented and set high goals, with short, medium, and long-term benchmarks to measure success.

12. **Self-management:** Successful entrepreneurs are self-starters. They don't need anyone to stay on top of them to ensure that things get done; they are self-motivated to take action and see all necessary tasks to completion. They can kick-start their own activity and then manage themselves effectively.

NOTES

Chapter 3

IMAGINATION: CAN YOU SEE IT?

"Imagination is more important than knowledge. For knowledge is limited, whereas imagination embraces the entire world, stimulating progress, giving birth to evolution."
-Albert Einstein

Imagination is a powerful force that enables people to innovate and be creative. It's something that every trailblazer must cultivate; it's the very ground on which they will thrive in their respective endeavors to create new strategies, blueprints, systems, ideas, inventions, products, and ministries, etc. It is no surprise that Albert Einstein said that imagination is more important than knowledge. Moving according to knowledge helps us stay on a safe track and operate according to predictable outcomes. Imagination challenges us to push beyond the status quo, giving way to major breakthroughs in our field.

Kingdom trailblazers are people of courage and vision. They chart a course into unknown territory with a bold imagination in order to accomplish what others believed could not be done. Even when they encounter challenges along the road, there is always a way forward with a fresh perspective on the landscape.

Leonardo da Vinci is one of the most notable polymaths in history. He is renowned for his paintings, such as the Mona Lisa and the Last Supper. But he was more than a painter; he was also a sculptor, architect, scientist, engineer, inventor, and anatomist. He had a vivid imagination that led to great innovations in science, technology, and engineering. He produced incredible inventions, models, and blueprints.

Leonardo da Vinci's fascination with the world around him, along with his imaginative mind, propelled him to create inventions that included a parachute, scuba gear, and sketches of a helicopter, tank, robot arm, and a watercraft.

Like da Vinci, a Kingdom trailblazer uses his or her imagination as a tool to solve problems and create new realities. Visionaries see possibilities that others overlook or may not yet see; they always look at things from different angles with an open mind. Their imagination enables them to push outside the confines of what already exists.

Here are five simple ways to cultivate your imagination so that you can begin to forge a path to the next frontier of discovery, creativity, and innovation in your field:

1. **Create a vision board:** You cultivate your imagination by exploring it in an intentional way that allows you to create mental pictures of the new realities that can be brought into existence. One of the best ways to do this is through a vision board where you create collages or images of what you would like to accomplish or produce. From there, you can begin to create a blueprint to manifest your imagination and goals in the real world.
2. **Walk:** A walk may be all you need to unleash the potential of your imagination. A study by Stanford in 2014 found that creativity increased by an average of 60% when walking. Many innovators already had this figured out long before science confirmed it; they would walk to stimulate their minds to produce fresh ideas. It is said that when inventor Nikola Tesla went out on long walks, he would often envision inventions, seeing every detail and solving every potential problem in his mind well before any physical experimentations.

3. **Read:** One of the best ways to cultivate imagination is by reading a good book. Reading is one of the best ways to stimulate the imagination because it introduces new thoughts, ideas, and perspectives. Established by many psychologists, reading has also been found to strengthen the mind. The brain acts like a muscle where it can be exercised and strengthened. Reading lets us visualize what we've read with words on paper describing specific images that readers must then manipulate inside their own minds. This strengthens our mental capacity just like any other form of exercising does for physical strength.

4. **Pray:** There is a supernatural side to innovation and receiving fresh ideas and new perspectives. When you're on a Kingdom assignment, God will sometimes take hold of your imagination and give you "revelation knowledge" to facilitate the process and help you bring about the results that He desires. In Acts 10:9-35, we see the apostle Peter praying around noon. While in prayer, he fell into a trance and received a revelation from God that revolutionized his outlook on Gentiles and his theology on their salvation. By a divine arresting of Peter's imagination, he saw and understood that Gentiles were also

favored by God and were welcomed into His Kingdom. So, he preached the Gospel to a group of Gentiles that sent for him; they were all filled with the Holy Spirit and baptized in Jesus' name!

5. **Dream Big:** One of the best ways to cultivate your imagination is to dream big. Dream without reservations or limitations. Dream without worrying about the technical aspects of your vision, such as how you're going to execute it or the resources you'll need. Allow yourself to create, explore, and imagine without limits; this will help you uncover new realities that can't be seen from where you are now. You don't need to have all the solutions to see possibilities. Once you see the possibilities in your mind, you can begin to strategize on making them a reality.

Your imagination is the incubator for life-changing, culture-shifting ideas. The mind is a powerful thing and what it imagines, it desires to create. So, get your imagination fired up and push the limits of what's possible! It's the first step in bringing your dreams to reality. And that's what a Kingdom pioneer does—they see possibilities and bring them into existence!

NOTES

Chapter 4

CREATIVITY

"Creativity doesn't wait for that perfect moment. It fashions its own perfect moments out of ordinary ones."
-Bruce Garrabrandt

Kingdom trailblazers have not only a vivid imagination but also creativity. Creativity is the use of the imagination to generate ideas or possibilities that can be utilized to solve problems or produce various works.

Linda Naiman eloquently states, "Creativity is the act of turning new and imaginative ideas into reality. Creativity is characterized by the ability to perceive the world in new ways, to find hidden patterns, to make connections between seemingly unrelated phenomena, and to generate solutions. Creativity involves two processes: thinking, then producing. If you have ideas but don't act on them, you are imaginative but not creative."

As a Kingdom pioneer, it is not enough for you to be imaginative and come up with great ideas; you must be a creative force who takes massive action to bring those dreams and ideas into reality. Only then can you be a trailblazing change agent for the Kingdom of God.

Bezalel is a great biblical example of a trailblazing Kingdom creative. Bezalel was a master craftsman whom God commissioned to lead the designing and building of a new structure where the Presence of God would dwell along with all of its furnishings and articles:

> *"Then Moses said to the sons of Israel, 'See, the Lord has called by name Bezalel the son of Uri, the son of Hur, of the tribe of Judah. And He has filled him with the Spirit of God, in wisdom, in understanding, in knowledge, and in all craftsmanship; to create designs for working in gold, in silver, and in bronze, and in the cutting of stones for settings and in the carving of wood, so as to perform in every inventive work'"*
> (Exodus 35:30-33 NASB).

Bezalel was anointed by the Holy Spirit with a special grace to perform in every inventive work. To be inventive means to have the ability to design or create new things or to think originally. As a trailblazer, your inventiveness will help you develop new ideas and possibilities that can bring practical solutions, shift culture and bring the Kingdom of God to bear in your sphere of influence.

Bezalel is the first person in Scripture noted as being filled with the Holy Spirit. This infilling of the Holy Spirit infused him with supernatural wisdom and creativity to bring a divine vision to life. When we think about being empowered by the Holy Spirit to do Kingdom work, it's usually things such as prophesying, healing the sick or casting out demons that come to mind. However, Bezalel's ministry is a great Scriptural example of how the Holy Spirit also empowers us for creative endeavors that make practical contributions to society. This is why Scripture says, *"whatever you do, work at it with all your heart, as working for the Lord, not for human masters"* (Colossians 3:23, NIV). Whether you're a construction worker, janitor, schoolteacher or CEO, the Holy Spirit can empower you like Bezalel to excel in your work, while serving a greater purpose.

When it comes to creativity, God is the ultimate Source: "For by Him all things were created that are in heaven and that are on earth, visible and invisible, whether thrones or dominions or principalities or powers. All things were created through Him and for Him" (Colossians 1:16, NKJV). Therefore, to increase creativity, we need to increase our intake of God's word, spend more time in prayer and cultivate a close relationship with Him. When we are fully connected to the Source, we will overflow with His creative power. Ask God to open up your creative potential and release new dreams, ideas and possibilities into your heart — ask Him for the knowledge, wisdom and understanding necessary to bring them to fruition.

Four Enemies of Creativity

The enemy does not want us to be creative. When we are creative, new ideas and innovations emerge that can depopulate the kingdom of darkness and populate the Kingdom of Heaven. The enemy will send fierce opposition to challenge Kingdom trailblazers and frustrate their plans. We must remain vigilant and deal with them swiftly and decisively so that the plans and purposes of God prevail.

Here are four major enemies to creativity against which we must guard:

#1 *Distraction*

Distraction is an enemy of creativity. The modern world is full of distractions. We have all sorts of entertainment at our fingertips; from video games to social media and streaming videos. And the internet provides endless opportunities for procrastination: surfing the web, reading blogs or checking our newsfeeds—all without any particular goal in mind other than killing time. These activities stifle creativity because they take up a great deal of time and mental energy that could otherwise be used to think creatively, produce new ideas, develop action plans and get things done.

Distractions cause us to lose focus and forget what our original intentions were. It can be very easy to get distracted from your calling in life by the many demands placed on you each day—family pressures, television programming, internet distractions, or the temptations of the world. Distractions can come in any form and are usually specific to each individual. But as Kingdom pioneers, we must be careful not to allow these things to impede our progress.

To be successful in your pursuits, you must overcome these distractions. It will require discernment, discipline, and self-control. You must be intentional about how you spend your time. You should have a clear purpose and goal for what you're doing at all times and remove anything from your life that prevents you from reaching those goals. Hebrews 12:1 admonishes us to "throw off everything that hinders and the sin that so easily entangles," and to "run with perseverance the race marked out for us."

Now, don't get me wrong, we all need time for R&R (rest and relaxation) to decompress and rejuvenate ourselves. However, it's also important to set reasonable boundaries for your downtime—for example, limiting the number of TV shows per week, or the hours spent on social media, etc.

#2 Self-doubt

The second enemy of creativity is self-doubt. Self-doubt will paralyze you and keep you from taking the risks necessary to create something new or accomplish great things for the Kingdom. You may think you're not good enough, smart enough, or talented enough to produce anything worthwhile—yet in reality, it's just your lack of faith that's hindering you.

Self-doubt is fortified when we compare ourselves to others. It's easy for people to see someone else as more talented, intelligent, or creative because they are not experiencing the same levels of success or productivity. But instead of comparing yourself to others, it's more beneficial to compare yourself to who you were 24 hours ago. Look in the mirror and ask yourself if you're doing everything within your power to improve and be successful. If you're not, then make some adjustments and do whatever it takes to get on the right track—for your sake as well as the Kingdom's.

Refuse to allow self-doubt to discourage you from achieving your dreams and goals. God has given you a unique set of gifts to fulfill your destiny. Believe in yourself and what God has placed inside of you. Then, when you are operating according to the will of God and are in alignment with His purpose for your life, you will not fail!

Moses struggled with self-doubt. Because of a speech impediment, he did not feel qualified to go before the Pharaoh and deliver God's message. God promised Moses that He would be with him and teach him what to say. The God that was with Moses and gave him success in his mission is the same God who is with you and will cause the work you do for Him to flourish.

#3 Procrastination

Procrastination is another way that creativity is stifled. Procrastination means putting off or delaying an action to a later time. Procrastination stifles creativity because creativity must not only imagine — it must also produce. The root word of creativity is "create," and to create means to bring something into existence. There are many reasons why people procrastinate:

- **Feeling overwhelmed** — When people feel overwhelmed, they will often do nothing or procrastinate. The best way to remedy this is to break down large tasks into smaller, more manageable ones. This will help you to find a sense of accomplishment and build momentum.

- **Perfectionism** — Perfectionism is when one feels that they can't produce anything good unless it's perfect. This mindset leads to fear of failure, idea stagnation, and procrastination. Mark Cuban, the billionaire entrepreneur and media proprietor, said, "Perfection is the enemy of profitability." There may never be a time on this side of Heaven where you will be 100% perfect. You need to get out there and take risks, endure ridicule, make mistakes, fail spectacularly at times — and then learn from it all to bring your vision into reality.
- **Vague or undefined goals** — When your goals are not clearly defined, it can cause you to feel overwhelmed and to procrastinate. This is because you may not know what you're supposed to do or how to do it. Without a roadmap or plan of action, you'll feel lost and will not know where to start. The best way to deal with this is to create a detailed plan with clearly-defined goals. Your goals should be specific and measurable so that the steps you need to take are

crystal-clear. Doing this will help give you a good sense of direction and purpose, ensuring that you are always moving forward towards the next step.

- **Lack of knowledge** — The lack of sufficient information may lead people to procrastinate because it is difficult to know how to go about the task at hand. The best way around this is to remain in a constant state of learning so that you can become more knowledgeable about what is required of you. Seek out a mentor as well — having someone in your corner who can help guide you can prove to be invaluable.
- **Lack of skills** — You may not produce anything because you don't have the skills required to bring your vision to life. A Kingdom trailblazer should never stop learning and growing. You may need to get more training and build your skills in order to produce your desired results. You may also need to delegate some tasks to those who have the skills that you lack.

#4 Fear

Fear is an enemy of creativity because it prevents the mind from moving beyond its comfort zone. Most groundbreaking discoveries are made in uncharted territories beyond the comfort zone, where the mind is open to new possibilities.

Fear of failure or fear of being embarrassed can stop us from being creative and acting. When we are afraid, our mind becomes overwhelmed with negative thoughts about what might happen if things don't turn out as planned. Then, we develop a lackadaisical attitude preventing us from being diligent and productive.

Proverbs 12:24 says, "Diligent hands will rule." We need to recognize fear for what it is—a tactic of the enemy designed to keep us from putting in the hard work that will bring success to our Kingdom endeavors. When you become aware of where your fears are coming from, you can begin to pull them out from their roots.

Fear is a liar! It will tell us that we cannot do something when the truth is that anything is possible with God's strength and provision!

One effective way to overcome the fear of failure is to develop a new perspective. Achieving great success in life means taking risks and being willing to make mistakes. Unfortunately, our society is quick to judge people for their failures. Still, those who succeed brilliantly often have failed disastrously but refused to quit and continued exploring new ideas or following the vision in their hearts.

As a creative, you must realize that God wastes no experience. Even being wrong is a valuable tool for the creative person. It helps us find out in which direction to go (or not go) and can lead us to groundbreaking discoveries and accomplishments. How many times have scientists failed at doing what they set their mind to, but through this process, found something even more valuable than the original goal?

The discovery of penicillin in 1928 by bacteriologist Alexander Fleming is one of the most significant moments in history as doctors now have an effective tool to cure their patients of life-threatening bacterial infections—and he discovered it entirely by accident.

Dr. Fleming was actually studying a bacteria called Staphylococcus, which causes sore throats and abscesses. One day after a vacation, he looked in a petri dish containing the bacteria and noticed mold growing in it. Upon further examination, he observed that no bacteria were growing in the immediate zone near the mold.

After a few weeks of further examination, he was not only intrigued by its inhibiting effect on bacteria, but also how it could be used as an antibiotic to combat infectious diseases like pneumonia and meningitis.

Dr. Fleming famously wrote: *"When I woke up just after dawn on September 28, 1928, I certainly didn't plan to revolutionize all medicine by discovering the world's first antibiotic, or bacteria killer. But I guess that was exactly what I did."*

As a Kingdom trailblazer, you must expel the spirit of fear, learn to enjoy the journey, and be open to exciting revelations and discoveries that can be uncovered as you move forward in your purpose.

Faith Over Fear

Faith is needed to fuel our creativity when fear tries to hinder it. Fear immobilizes, but faith propels you forward into an exciting and fulfilling future! Faith releases creative energy within you that will help you to reach your full potential in Christ.

Jesus said, "Humanly speaking, it is impossible. But with God everything is possible" (Matthew 19:26 NLT). The Kingdom pioneer must have the faith that makes it possible for God to work through them and on their behalf. The stronger your faith, the greater your creativity will be! You'll begin seeing and working toward what could be instead of only seeing what is—and that's when the true power of a Kingdom trailblazer will be unleashed!

NOTES

Chapter 5

TRAILBLAZING FAITH

Trailblazing faith is required to complete a God-sized task or launch out into the unknown and attempt what has never been accomplished. Pioneers must develop a strong faith as they are often called to go into places that others won't. They have to possess an unwavering faith that will help secure victory in their pursuits. The Word of God says, *"And this is the victory that has overcome the world – our faith"* (1 John 5:4, NKJV). When your faith is fortified by prayer and the Word of God, it becomes an impenetrable force that produces an assuredness in your efforts to achieve your objectives and reach your goals. Faith is a strong foundation for any endeavor, and trailblazers must be grounded on it as they take risks to accomplish great things. Faith will carry you through the unknown with the assurance that God is with you to make your impact felt and to help you succeed.

Many Kingdom trailblazers will also operate in the gift of faith, one of the nine spiritual gifts listed in the twelfth chapter of 1 Corinthians. The gift of faith unlocks the door for miracles to manifest. Miracles and supernatural breakthroughs occur when trailblazers are able to see beyond the limitations of today and into the realm of God's possibilities. From there, they tap into the power of faith and move boldly into what God has destined them to accomplish. Faith becomes a force to be reckoned with when activated amid a trial or crisis, and it has the power to change a situation, open up closed doors, and bring victory in adverse conditions.

When we trust God wholeheartedly, step out of the boat, and dare to walk on water like Peter, we open ourselves up to discover unexpected new insights from the Spirit of God, which can lead us forward to accomplish the extraordinary!

Do you believe that God has purposed you to achieve something more significant than what you have done so far? Do you believe that He's anointed you to slay "giants" in your field and make a difference in your generation? Consider young David the shepherd boy:

No one believed that David was able to defeat Goliath. When David told King Saul that he would take on the giant, King Saul said, "You are not able to go out against this Philistine and fight him; you are only a young man, and he has been a warrior from his youth" (1 Samuel 17:33, NIV).

Young David did not allow the king's words to instill fear or self-doubt within himself. He knew what God placed inside of him and had an impenetrable faith that the anointing on his life was more than enough to meet the challenge. David then said to King Saul:

> *"Your servant has been keeping his father's sheep. When a lion or a bear came and carried off a sheep from the flock, I went after it, struck it and rescued the sheep from its mouth. When it turned on me, I seized it by its hair, struck it and killed it. Your servant has killed both the lion and the bear; this uncircumcised Philistine will be like one of them because he has defied the armies of the living God. The Lord who rescued me from the paw of the lion and the paw of the bear will rescue me from the hand of this Philistine"* (1 Samuel 17:34-37, NIV).

David achieved a great victory for Israel that day and instantly rose to fame and fortune. This great victory would also set the stage for David eventually becoming the king of Israel.

In like manner, you have no time to entertain the negative words of naysayers. You must be confident in what God has placed inside of you. Even amidst doubt and strong opposition, you must possess unshakeable faith, fully persuaded that the Lord will grant you success in your Kingdom endeavors.

Developing Trailblazing Faith

Here are 6 ways to develop the trailblazing faith needed to move mountains, overcome obstacles, and succeed on a Kingdom scale:

1. Hearing the Word of God

Romans 10:17 says, *"So then faith comes by hearing, and hearing by the word of God"* (NKJV). Your hearing faculty is a gateway to your inner being. What goes through the ear gate can take root in the soul (mind, will, and emotions) and spirit (see Matthew 13:1-35, the parable of the sower). The more you expose yourself to the word of God, the deeper it takes root within you, nurturing, strengthening, and reinforcing your faith.

On the opposite side of the spectrum, it may also be necessary to disconnect from and uproot the negative voices in your life. These voices release words over you to limit your ability to operate in faith and live beyond the natural. These voices can come from within or without; it's your job to silence them and make room for the word of truth.

It is important to note that the Greek rendering of "word" in Romans 10:17 is rehma. A rehma word is a living word from the mouth of God that carries power and life (see Hebrews 4:12). It is a divine utterance from God that has implications for a particular situation. When you receive a rehma, it will change how your mind thinks, your decisions, and how you approach life. In order to experience greater faith, you must allow the rehma to take root within you and align your heart, mind, and spirit with the word that has been spoken to you.

The rehma can come to you in many ways: reading and meditating on the Holy Scriptures, through visions and dreams or a prophetic word, etc.

2. *Understanding the Word*

Understanding means to have clear insight and grasp the true meaning or importance of something. For faith to grow by hearing the word of God, you must also understand what you are hearing. In the parable of the sower in Matthew chapter 13, the word of God is likened to a seed that is sown into the heart of the hearer. When the hearer did not understand the word, the enemy came and snatched the seed so that it would not take root. Therefore, as you hear the word of God, take the time to grasp its meaning and implication for your life to ensure that the seed takes root and grows. Otherwise, it can be quickly snatched away by the enemy.

3. *Confessing and Declaring*

Your words are powerful! They have the power to bring things into existence. When you make a declaration, you verbally assert that something is so. Declarations not only help to release faith in you, but they also have the capacity to bring about change in the spiritual and natural realms.

When you confess the word, you come into agreement with what the word of God has already declared. And when you're aligned with God and what He has spoken, your faith is activated to see those things come to pass.

4. *Exercise*

Faith is like a muscle; you must exercise it in order for it to grow strong. You exercise your faith by acting on the revealed word and will of God. This is a daily discipline that you must practice consistently. Faith and obedience go hand in hand (see Romans chapter 1). As you exercise your faith by obeying God's word and His revealed will for your life, you can expect to see breakthroughs, miracles, and answered prayers.

5. Fasting and Prayer

Another key element to developing trailblazing faith is fasting and praying. Fasting coupled with prayer supercharges your spiritual senses and capabilities (see Matthew 17: 18-21). You will have a stronger connection to God, hear His voice more clearly, and have a greater depth of understanding. Fasting and prayer connect to hearing and understanding the rehma, fueling and strengthening your faith even more.

6. Hearing the Testimonies of Others

Faith can increase by hearing the testimonies of other individuals who overcame tremendous obstacles by exercising their faith. Hearing about other Kingdom trailblazers who have achieved great success by applying their faith can instill a greater sense of confidence in you to step out in faith, believing that you can experience similar results.

NOTES

Chapter 6

RISK TAKERS

"Faith is spelled R-I-S-K"
-Chris Overstreet

Kingdom Trailblazers are courageous people with a sense of adventure and an intense passion for their work. They understand that they must take risks to achieve their goals. Although there may be setbacks and failures, they know that they'll eventually reach their destination if they don't quit.

Faith is spelled R-I-S-K. In order to innovate, achieve breakthroughs, and defeat giants in your field, you must take risks. You cannot "play it safe" or use only tried and true methods when you know that these won't bring about the desired results. You must be willing to venture out into the unknown, step out in faith, and take calculated risks.

Many people are so afraid to take a risk that they fail to pursue the call on their lives. Instead, they limit themselves, never exploring the possibilities of what could be. As a result, they become stuck in a rut, living a life of mediocrity.

Apple Inc. started in a garage with $1,300 in working capital and no prior experience building and marketing computers. It rose from humble beginnings to become the world's most valuable company. One of the company's co-founders, Steve Jobs, is a household name. Many people are also acquainted with another co-founder, Steve Wozniak, who served as an electronics engineer and computer scientist. However, there's another founder, Ronald Wayne, who is considerably less well-known.

Ronald Wayne was a friend of Jobs from his time at Atari. Jobs brought him on board to provide stability to the company because he was much older and had more business experience. Jobs also saw him as one who could mediate between him and Wozniak if they should have any disagreements. One day the three co-founders met at Wayne's apartment where he drafted up their partnership agreement. Wayne's primary responsibilities included Mechanical Engineering and Documentation.

After twelve days, Ron Wayne decided that he didn't want to risk being personally liable for the company's debts should it fail and sold his 10% stake back to Jobs and Wozniak for

$800. Soon after he received $1,500 more totaling $2,300. Had Wayne stayed on board and taken the risk, his 10% stake would have eventually made him a multi-billionaire. Instead, he chose to play it safe and walk away from what could have been the opportunity of a lifetime.

When you take risks, there's always the potential for failure. However, if you don't take risks, you will never achieve anything great. Consider the words of Jim Rohn:

> *"It's all risky. The minute you were born it got risky. If you think trying is risky, wait till they hand you the bill for not trying."*

Jeff Bezos, the founder of the multinational e-commerce company, Amazon, is one of the most innovative and successful people in history. In the tech boom of the 1990s, Jeff Bezos discovered and served an untapped market by delivering one's reading experience to their doorstep without them having to leave their house to shop. He revolutionized how people buy, sell, and read books. His company was also one the first to offer a wide range of products for sale online that could be shipped directly to the customer's door within days. Amazon eventually became a household name with its ability to dispatch any product from any place all over the world directly to our homes.

Bezos dared to believe in his ambitions and pursued his vision. He left behind the security of working as a V.P. at a firm on Wall Street for an unfamiliar world: the world of technology and entrepreneurship—with cutting-edge ideas, a new model for doing business online —and a lot of uncertainty. It was a risky move to leave the comforts of his job, but he took a risk in the belief that he could make this bold move, pursue his entrepreneurial passions, and build a profitable company from scratch.

Even though there were many uncertainties about what could happen if things didn't go well, Jeff took a chance. He believed that he could make it work and that the rewards would be worth any potential challenges. It was so risky that he warned early investors that there was up to a 70% chance of losing all of their money.

Well, just a few years after starting Amazon in his garage, Jeff Bezos became a billionaire. Today, Amazon is one of the largest and most successful companies in the world. And after 24 years of founding it, Bezos became the wealthiest person in the world, with a net worth of approximately $200 billion. So, what does that say about how risk-taking can pay off?

Calculated Risks

A calculated risk is different from a reckless one. A calculated risk has a higher probability of success because it's approached with wisdom, research, and strategic planning. Of course, you should not take risks just for the sake of doing so. But when a risk is a necessity and in alignment with your values, vision, and mission, then it's worth taking.

Innovation and risk are inseparable. It's a delicate balance between risk and reward. No matter how carefully you plan, no venture is guaranteed to succeed in the way you've imagined — that's what makes it so exciting! Pioneers take their ideas into uncharted territory where success can't be predicted with 100% accuracy. From high-risk startups to expanding service offerings within your business, or starting a cutting-edge ministry to reach an underserved demographic, every move holds an element of uncertainty, but it also entails opportunities for great rewards if things go well!

While some people opt to risk nothing to protect time, money, and other resources, Kingdom pioneers are willing to step out of their comfort zones and beyond the familiar for an idea that they believe has the potential to impact society in unique ways.

Here are 5 steps for taking calculated risks:

1. **Be sure it's from God:** Kingdom trailblazers should always seek the Lord for direction before moving forward because they want the best possible outcomes. This is where godly wisdom, counsel and discernment come into play.
2. **Research:** To make a good decision, you must go through it with a fine-tooth comb. The more information you have for the decision-making process, the lower the risk and the greater your likelihood of success. Investigate all details involved and be aware of red flags that might pop up before they happen so you can steer clear of any avoidable problems down the line.
3. **Develop an action plan:** Make sure you have a specific goal in mind along with an attainable deadline to accomplish it. List out each step necessary to achieve your objectives and break it down into manageable milestones. Understand what success looks like so you can quickly recognize if your actions are taking you in that direction.
4. **Anticipate obstacles:** Consider things that could go wrong and make contingency plans in case they do. Consider the worst-case scenarios and how you will

deal with them. Be as prepared to overcome these obstacles as possible, but still be flexible with your approach.

5. **Adjust your strategy accordingly:** Realize when things aren't going how you anticipated and take time to re-strategize—then try again! Persevere in faith through good times and bad, knowing that Kingdom risk-taking will change lives around you.

NOTES

Chapter 7

TEAM-BUILDING

"The smartest man in the room surrounds himself, in that same room, with people, who are smarter than he."
-Henry Ford

Teamwork is a powerful force. Teams are not just groups of people who have been given assigned tasks. They are something more; individuals come together and create a new entity with a synergy that is greater than the sum of its parts. A team can achieve things that no individual could on their own.

When team members get together for brainstorming sessions, the energy in the room has an electric charge to it. Every individual's intelligence compounds with everyone else's, so you end up having this tsunami wave of creativity. However, this creative synergy doesn't happen all by itself; there needs to be someone at the helm guiding everything—someone who knows how to manage complexity (and chaos) without losing sight of what really matters: getting things done. This person is you — the Kingdom trailblazer!

If you desire to achieve your goals and dreams, you're going to need a team to support you. But not just any team — you'll need the right people with skills and abilities that compliment your own. You need to surround yourself with like-minded individuals that share your passion, vision, and values.

Kingdom pioneers must become master team builders. They must become savvy about people and be able to manage different personalities with varying levels of skill sets, experience, and IQs. They need to be able to assemble teams that can create solutions to problems or complete a task in the most efficient way possible.

For example, an entrepreneur might come up with an idea for a new product and then assemble a team of developers, marketers, and other specialists to work on it. A missionary might come up with a new method to connect with distant communities in a way that facilitates their preaching of the Gospel and winning souls. They will assemble a team of financiers, intercessors, and local leaders from those communities, and will harvest hands to help execute a particular strategy or plan.

Kingdom trailblazers believe in team effort because they know how difficult it is for one person to do everything alone. The trailblazer can't do the job without his team members, so they must make sure that every member has a place on the team to make a valuable contribution and show them appreciation, honor, and mutual respect.

To excel at building and leading a team, you must have the ability to evaluate all of those around you and see their strengths. Then you must display confident leadership that motivates others to use their diverse skills to benefit a common goal.

An exceptional team builder effortlessly and effectively guides, inspires, and mentors people to help them reach their full potential and accomplish what they couldn't do independently. Here are eleven more qualities that you should develop to be a more effective team builder and leader:

1. **Good Communication Skills** — Communication is a two-way street, and the best leaders are those who know how to convey their goals in an understandable fashion, while also being able to listen and hear the concerns and ideas of others. They can take constructive criticism from their team members without it affecting their confidence or self-esteem.

They give constructive criticism that builds up rather than tears down.

2. **Empathy** — A team builder needs to understand the struggles of their teammates and provide support and encouragement to help them grow and thrive. They can't do this if they don't feel what their team members are feeling, so it's important to be empathetic.
3. **Punctuality** — The ability of a leader to respect time is one of their most essential qualities. Team builders are aware of how precious time is and know its value in order to accomplish goals, so they make sure to keep a tight schedule and maintain their commitments.
4. **Strategic Planning** — Team builders know that good planning is needed for things to get done with minimal setbacks. Team builders plan out all the steps that need to be taken to achieve a goal and then delegate those tasks to the appropriate people.
5. **Delegation** — According to John C. Maxwell, "If you want to do a few small things right, do them yourself. If you want to do great things and make a big impact, learn to delegate." An exceptional team builder is a master delegator. They entrust responsibilities to team members in a way that drives productivity and achieves success. A good team builder will not micro-

manage their team. They will empower qualified individuals to participate in critical decision-making and trust them to use their judgment and skills to complete the assigned tasks.

6. **Recruiting Skills** — Team builders can evaluate potential and enlist qualified people into their ranks. They do this in a compelling and welcoming way, and they make sure to find the right people that will work well together. They're able to assess someone's strengths, engage them in conversation, and find out what they can do. From there, they offer an invitation and persuade the potential team member to join them. A good team builder can also recruit without saying a word. When people with like passions see what they're doing and how they're doing it, they'll want to join them.

7. **Positive Attitude** — Team builders have a positive attitude and the things that they do reflect it. They're able to look at things from a different perspective, think outside of the box, and remain good-natured even when faced with adversity or opposition. A team builder's positivity inspires others by example.

8. **Motivation** — Team builders galvanize their team to work together as a unit and accomplish the task at hand. They do this in a way that the team members

feel valued and respected, inspiring them to do the very best that they can.

9. **Initiative**—Successful team builders set the example and lead the charge forward. They are not afraid to take action. They work with their team and act quickly on the challenges or opportunities that arise—they're proactive rather than reactive.
10. **Vision Casting**—Great team builders cast a vision in a way that inspires others to follow their lead. They know how to articulate their goals in a manner that makes people want to be part of the journey. They effectively communicate the team's goal in a way that is perceived as achievable and worthwhile.
11. **Self-Confidence**—No one will follow someone who is insecure and unsure of their abilities. A team builder who lacks confidence will lack the ability to lead others and initiate change, which is a huge disadvantage in any organization. A good team builder is self-confident. This is in contrast to being prideful, which means being arrogant and unapproachable. Team builders are confident in their skills, abilities, strengths—and weaknesses. This self-confidence also helps them take ownership of their mistakes, learn from them, and grow as a person to be better in the future. Team members appreciate

confident vulnerability and transparency and are more likely to stick it out with the team through major setbacks or when the goals have to be adjusted.

Team building is an essential skill to master. When Kingdom trailblazers effectively assemble and equip teams to achieve a particular objective, the outcome will be success and victory. Their efforts are well-rewarded as the Kingdom advances.

NOTES

Chapter 8

LEGACY: LAYING THE FOUNDATION FOR FUTURE GENERATIONS

"Momentum cannot be achieved without motion. To put things in motion, a foundation must be laid first."
-Cory Mosley

The importance of a Kingdom trailblazer is not just in their accomplishments but also in the legacy they leave behind for future generations to build upon. When a person dies, that individual's legacy lives on. However, legacy is not just about the inheritance an individual leaves behind; it also encompasses what they've achieved in life and how much of their good qualities will live on in the hearts and minds of others. The story of one's life reflects their entire existence — including accomplishments, the impact left on others, and the hardships faced and overcome along their journey.

A strong foundation provides stability and a measure of predictability even as circumstances change, making it easier for others to continue building and advancing. Leaving a solid foundation is an important part of the work we do as ambassadors for Christ. We don't dwell too long on the past, marveling or reminiscing over previous achievements. Instead, we continue to push forward, strengthening the foundation, so the work continues on creating a chain reaction of innovation, breakthrough, and progress for succeeding generations.

Intentional Legacy

It should be intentional for your work or influence to live on through someone else. Being intentional about your legacy means that you plan how others will carry on your work in advance.

The first step is to look inside and gain a thorough understanding of your life's purpose and mission. This gives us a starting point to develop an intentional legacy — a track we want others to follow as they continue our calling into new territory.

Next, you must identify those individuals who share your vision and values, and who are capable and willing to pick up the mantle and carry on the work. Paul and Titus are excellent illustrations of this point:

In the epistle of Titus, the apostle Paul instructs his apostolic understudy Titus to remain in Crete and appoint elders in every town. He also instructs Titus to "...*set them an example by doing what is good. In your teaching show integrity, seriousness and soundness of speech that cannot be condemned, so that those who oppose you may be ashamed because they have nothing bad to say about us*" (Titus 2:7-8, NIV).

Paul's instruction to Titus is a clear example of intentional legacy. Paul made sure that Titus was empowered and equipped to take on the work and responsibilities he had started before he left.

Lastly, you must set up a process to hand over your vision and values so they can be communicated from one person to the next in an efficient way that is tailored to their skill sets.

The Lasting Legacy of Florence Nightingale

Florence Nightingale is another Kingdom pioneer who impacted the world outside the four walls of the Church. She was a statistician, social reformer, and the mother of modern nursing.

Nightingale was born in 1820 into a British aristocratic family. As a young lady, she was given every advantage of an upper-class upbringing; however, she defied expectations by not marrying wealthy, and pursued a career in nursing against her parents' wishes. She believed it was her divine purpose.

During the Crimean War, at the behest of Secretary of War Sidney Herbert, Nightingale recruited and trained nurses from various religious orders, and they cared for wounded soldiers. She was nicknamed "The Lady with the Lamp" for how she cared for soldiers at night. Others called her "The Angel of the Crimea," as she reduced the hospital's death rate by two thirds!

In 1860, Florence founded the Nightingale Training School for Nurses. This was groundbreaking as it was the first school of nursing in the world and set an international precedent. Today there are approximately 1,500 schools of nursing worldwide.

Like Nightingale, as Kingdom trailblazers, we must know our purpose and pursue it with tenacity—even if it means disappointing others who expect us to follow in traditional footsteps. We must maintain a standard of excellence that communicates our faith to others, and we must use our gifts in a way that makes the most of who God has made us to be.

And while continuing our pioneering efforts, we must entrust others with our objectives, vision, and values so that they can carry on the work beyond us. Intentional legacy is about leaving a lasting impression on the world and empowering others to do the same.

What will your legacy be?

NOTES

CONCLUSION

An army of trailblazers is arising in the Kingdom for such a time as this. A fresh wave of courageous and innovative leaders are on the move, serving as creative catalysts for Kingdom breakthrough. There is nothing that will stop us from staying in motion! There will be great challenges, but it is worth every ounce of energy spent—the rewards outweigh the sacrifice.

The future is being shaped by Kingdom pioneers all over the globe. We must step into our purpose and pursue it with passion. We must become skilled in mobilizing people and resources to serve the mission and pay the price to see Kingdom breakthrough. It is time to break out of the box of mediocrity and live and lead in an extraordinary way.

When anointed pioneers and innovators are raised and released into society, the Kingdom will make a greater impact. The Church needs more Kingdom trailblazers who can design a blueprint to live and thrive in this new future.

No one has all of the answers, but there is power in numbers, and the collective wisdom of Christ's people will bring about a greater good.

It is time for the Kingdom pioneers to take their rightful place in the world — as leaders who leave an intentional legacy that lives on through others. It's time we start looking at things like mission statements, succession plans, and more, because this generation won't last forever, but our work and influence will.

Societal Transformation

The work that we do as Kingdom Trailblazers is an integral part of the overall process of shifting people's hearts and minds. When these are changed, it will impact the way society operates.

We are called to be innovators and leaders who will turn the tide of society. We are Kingdom trailblazers, and our impact will extend beyond borders — our collective works will affect the global community, and the Kingdom will come alive in ways we never imagined!

It is time for us to arise and answer the call to be change agents. We are not called to be thermometers who merely reflect the climate of society; we are to be thermostats who actively shape the climate of the environment where we live and work.

Kingdom pioneers should never be contained in anyone's box of traditional ways of doing things. Instead, we must be free to be ourselves and create new paths, systems, and paradigms that impact society. It is time to spark creativity, innovation, and change; it is time for us to blaze a trail that others will follow.

> *"Using a dull ax requires great strength, so sharpen the blade..."*
> (Ecclesiastes 10:10, NLT).

I encourage you, the reader, to sharpen your pioneering edge and release your creativity into society. Take up the mantle of a Kingdom trailblazer and do great exploits with your gifts, talents, and resources.

Mind What's in Your Own Bag

> *"To one he gave five bags of gold, to another two bags, and to another one bag, each according to his ability..."*
> (Matthew 25:15, NIV).

You may look at the characters used as examples in this book and feel that you may never accomplish what they have done, but do not compare yourself to anyone else. You're only responsible for what God has given and assigned to you.

The parable of the bags of gold illustrates how God gives us varying measures of resources and responsibilities. We were not all called to accomplish the same things on the same scale; rather, we each have a unique assignment and mission no one else can carry out. What's important is that you are faithful with what you have been given and are profitable to God.

Creating a Legacy of Leadership

Christian leadership in the 21st century is about making an intentional impact on culture that will live beyond our lifetimes. It's about leaving a powerful legacy to carry on after we are gone through our influence, impact, and accomplishments.

Thrust yourself out of your comfort zone and step boldly into your destiny. The reward of the Kingdom trailblazer shall be great. You will never regret accepting God's call to go forth and change the world.

Affirmations for the Kingdom Trailblazer

- I will not be contained in the box of traditional ways of doing things.
- I will break down barriers, shift paradigms, and make waves in society.
- I will take up the mantle of a Kingdom trailblazer and do great exploits with my gifts, talents, and resources.
- I will not be afraid to dream BIG and walk in my destiny!
- I will break the curse of poverty in my family and will live abundantly.
- I will be victorious over the obstacles of life through my faith in God and a relentless pursuit of my destiny.
- I will not let my past determine what I can accomplish in the present.
- I will be a force for good in my community and will leave my imprint on generations to come.
- My leadership will outlive me and change society in a significant way.
- I am faithful with what I have been given.
- I will break into new markets and release fresh ideas into society.

- I live in abundance and have the resources to help others.
- I will not be afraid to try something different and press into new territory.
- I will think boldly and creatively to see the needs of my generation met for the glory of God.
- I will live a life of adventure and excitement, seeking out new ways to fulfill my mission in life.
- I will break through into new territory and accomplish my goals with passion and excellence.
- I am creative and innovative in my approach to life, business, and ministry.
- I will not be restricted or paralyzed by doubt, fear, or unbelief.
- I will brazenly step out in faith into new territory never before explored or conquered.
- I will think and act outside the confines of traditional mindsets.
- I will be a trailblazer and pioneer in my family, community, and culture.
- I am a change agent who will shift paradigms, break barriers, and establish a Kingdom culture in my environment.
- I'm a pioneer that leaves a trail for others to follow.

- I will step out to accomplish things that others deem impossible, with trailblazing faith.
- I am adaptable and innovative in my approach to engage culture with the message of Christ and demonstration of the Kingdom.
- I'm a daring, visionary leader who dares to dream and push boundaries.
- I've been tested, purified by the Refiner's fire, and anointed to create change.
- My imagination is the incubator for life-changing, culture-shifting ideas to be birthed.
- I am a reformer who will not settle for the status quo or be satisfied with mediocrity.
- My creativity is the catalyst for reform, change, and progress.
- My imagination and creativity are ignited to create new ideas and strategies.
- I am a creative, innovative thinker who thrives on pushing the envelope and taking daring leaps to accomplish big things.
- I will relentlessly pursue excellence in all my endeavors.
- My creativity is an expression of God's Spirit at work in me.

- I am a visionary who can see beyond the present and into the future to create groundbreaking works.
- My imagination stretches the limits of possibilities.
- I will take calculated risks to break into new territory and accomplish my life's mission.
- I am a risk-taker who will not be governed by the fear of failure or the opinions of others.
- I will not be afraid of change but embrace it willingly to accomplish my mission.
- I will not be defined or limited by my past failures.
- My faith and passion propel me forward in pursuit of my dreams and aspirations.
- I will press past the limitations of people's opinions to achieve great things.
- I will not settle for anything less than God's best in every area of my life.
- I am confident in my skills, abilities, and strengths.
- I will take ownership of my mistakes and shortcomings, learn from them, and grow as a person and leader.

REFERENCES

giantsforgod.com, accessed May 15, 2022, www.giantsforgod.com/john-d-rockefeller-sr-standard-oil

Henry Louis Gates Jr., "Madam Walker, the First Black American Woman to Be a Self-Made Millionaire," www.pbs.org, accessed May 16, 2022, www.pbs.org/wnet/african-americans-many-rivers-to-cross/history/100-amazing-facts/madam-walker-the-first-black-american-woman-to-be-a-self-made-millionaire

Tim Haford, "The warrior monks who invented banking," bbc.com, accessed May 16th, 2022, https://www.bbc.com/news/business-38499883

Wikipedia, "Martin Luther," accessed May 12, 2022, https://en.wikipedia.org/wiki/Martin_Luther

Linda Naiman, "What is Creativity? (And why is it a crucial factor for business success?)," www.creativityatwork.com, accessed May 15, 2022

Made in the USA
Middletown, DE
13 March 2023